HOW ARE MICROCHIPS MADE?

A Storytelling Guide to the Science Behind ICs Manufacturing

Joe E. Grayson

Table of Contents

Introduction

Microchips are at the heart of the technological revolution, silently powering the tools and devices that define our modern lives. From the smartphones in our pockets to the supercomputers unraveling the mysteries of the universe, these tiny marvels of engineering have become indispensable. They are the unsung heroes of progress, enabling breakthroughs in medicine, communication, transportation, and countless other fields. Despite their ubiquity, the intricate process that goes into creating these chips often remains a mystery to the very people who rely on them daily.

Understanding how microchips are made is more than just a technical exploration; it is a window into the ingenuity and precision of human achievement. It sheds light on the collaboration of science, engineering, and craftsmanship required to build components that are measured in billionths of a meter. Delving into this world uncovers the sheer complexity of a process that spans months and involves hundreds of steps, all executed with nanometer-level accuracy. Appreciating this process not only deepens our respect for technology but also helps us grasp the challenges and triumphs involved in creating the systems that drive the modern age.

This book aims to unravel the mysteries of microchip manufacturing, presenting the information in a way that captures the imagination while maintaining accuracy and depth. Through a storytelling approach, it weaves a narrative that blends science and art, taking readers on a journey through the hidden world of semiconductor fabrication. It balances detailed analysis with engaging explanations, ensuring that the content is accessible and captivating for all readers, regardless of their technical background.

The pages ahead will offer a step-by-step exploration of how microchips are born, from the silicon wafer to the integrated circuits that bring our devices to life. Along the way, readers will encounter the machines, techniques, and principles that underpin this complex process, gaining a newfound appreciation for the marvels that make our digital world possible. This is a story not just about technology, but about the ingenuity and ambition that have shaped the way we live and work.

Chapter 1: The Hidden World of Microchips

Microchips, also known as integrated circuits, are tiny yet powerful electronic components that serve as the brain behind nearly every modern device. These chips are composed of billions of transistors intricately arranged on a wafer of silicon, enabling them to process data, perform calculations, and execute instructions with astonishing speed and precision. Their function is to control and manipulate electrical signals, making them essential for everything from the simplest household appliances to the most advanced supercomputers. Without microchips, the conveniences and capabilities of the digital age would simply not exist.

To understand their importance, imagine the device you're likely holding right now—a smartphone. Behind its sleek exterior lies an intricate network of microchips that powers its functionality. One chip might handle the processing tasks required for apps and games, another manages memory, while yet another ensures seamless communication over networks. Whether you're streaming a video, navigating via GPS, or chatting with friends, microchips are working tirelessly to make it all happen in real time.

Consider another everyday scenario: a modern car. Today's vehicles are equipped with microchips that control everything from the engine's performance to the safety systems like airbags and anti-lock brakes. These chips are even integral to the entertainment systems and advanced driver-assistance features that enhance convenience and safety on the road.

Microchips are not just limited to consumer devices. They are the cornerstone of industries like healthcare, enabling life-saving technologies such as MRI machines and robotic surgery. In aerospace, they guide satellites and spacecraft with unparalleled precision. They even play a pivotal role in powering the world's data centers, the unseen infrastructure that keeps the internet running.

The versatility and indispensability of microchips in modern life underscore their monumental importance. They are the silent workhorses behind the technology we depend on, driving innovation and shaping the way we live, work, and communicate. Through these examples, it becomes clear that microchips are not just components of technology; they are the foundation of the digital world.

The story of microchips begins with the rise of semiconductors, a transformative discovery that reshaped the trajectory of human innovation. In the early 20th century, scientists unraveled the unique properties of materials like silicon and germanium, which could act as both conductors and insulators under specific conditions. This dual nature gave birth to the field of semiconductor technology, paving the way for breakthroughs that would revolutionize electronics.

The journey toward integrated circuits, or ICs, started with the invention of the transistor in 1947 by John Bardeen, Walter Brattain, and William Shockley. This small device replaced bulky vacuum tubes, offering a more efficient and reliable way to amplify and switch electronic signals. It marked a paradigm shift, allowing devices to become smaller, faster, and more energy-efficient. By the 1950s, transistors were being manufactured at scale, but as circuits grew more complex, it became clear that assembling individual transistors and components manually was inefficient and limiting.

In 1958, Jack Kilby of Texas Instruments and Robert Noyce of Fairchild Semiconductor independently developed the first integrated circuits. These revolutionary devices combined multiple electronic components on a single piece of silicon, effectively creating the first microchips. Kilby's prototype demonstrated the feasibility of miniaturizing entire circuits, while Noyce's planar process refined the manufacturing techniques, making ICs commercially viable. Their work laid the foundation for the semiconductor industry and earned Kilby a Nobel Prize in Physics.

The 1960s and 1970s saw rapid advancements, driven by Moore's Law, the observation by Gordon Moore that the number of transistors on a chip would roughly double every two years. This principle became a guiding force for the industry, spurring relentless innovation and pushing the limits of miniaturization. By the 1980s, microchips had become the cornerstone of computing, powering the rise of personal computers and laying the groundwork for the digital age.

As microchips continued to evolve, their influence expanded into every corner of modern life. They became the essential building blocks for smartphones, the internet, artificial intelligence, and countless other technologies. The relentless march of semiconductor innovation transformed microchips from a novel invention into the driving force behind the digital revolution.

Today, microchips are the linchpin of the digital age. They enable the seamless flow of information, the automation of industries, and the connectivity that defines our world. Every digital interaction, from sending an email to navigating a spacecraft, is powered by the complex and precise operations of microchips. Their evolution embodies the essence of technological progress, making them not just a marvel of engineering but the foundation upon which the modern world stands.

Chapter 2: Inside the Silicon Factory

A semiconductor fabrication plant, commonly known as a fab, is a marvel of modern engineering and science, a place where the invisible becomes tangible. These factories are the birthplace of microchips, housing the intricate processes required to craft billions of transistors onto a wafer of silicon. Unlike typical manufacturing facilities, fabs are uniquely specialized, built to accommodate the extraordinary precision demanded by semiconductor production.

At the heart of every fab is the cleanroom, a meticulously controlled environment designed to minimize contamination. Even a single dust particle, invisible to the naked eye, can ruin a silicon wafer, rendering an entire batch of microchips unusable. For this reason, the cleanroom's air is constantly filtered to ensure purity levels thousands of times greater than those of a typical operating theater. Workers inside wear full-body suits, often referred to as "bunny suits," to prevent the tiniest particles from their skin or breath from contaminating the environment.

Cleanrooms are massive, often spanning the size of several football fields. This scale is necessary to accommodate the hundreds of highly specialized machines used in the manufacturing process. These machines range in size from that of a small van to a city bus and can cost anywhere from a few million to over $100 million each. Despite their size and complexity, they work with astonishing precision, executing processes at scales measured in nanometers.

The cost of constructing and equipping a modern semiconductor fab is staggering, often exceeding $10 billion. Much of this investment goes into ensuring the precision and cleanliness required for manufacturing at the atomic level. Every aspect of the cleanroom, from its temperature and humidity to the vibration control of its floors, is carefully regulated to support the delicate operations carried out within.

Precision is the cornerstone of a fab's operations. Silicon wafers move seamlessly from machine to machine, undergoing hundreds of intricate processes. Each step must be executed with nanometer-level accuracy, as even the slightest deviation can lead to defects. The machines inside a fab use cutting-edge technology, combining principles of physics, chemistry, and engineering to create the tiny structures that make up microchips.

Semiconductor fabrication plants are not just manufacturing facilities; they are testaments to human ingenuity and the relentless pursuit of perfection. These cleanrooms, where science and precision converge, serve as the stage for the creation of the microchips that power our digital world.

Inside the semiconductor fabrication plant, the machines are as much a marvel as the microchips they help create. These highly specialized tools, each designed for a specific function, operate in perfect harmony to transform raw silicon into a finished integrated circuit. The sheer variety of machines, each playing a critical role in the manufacturing process, showcases the complexity and precision of the operation.

The fab is home to six primary categories of machines, each corresponding to a distinct phase of production. Some machines are responsible for creating the mask layers, the stencils used to pattern the chip's intricate designs. These include photolithography tools, which shine ultraviolet light through photomasks to imprint patterns onto a wafer, and spin coaters, which apply the light-sensitive photoresist that captures these patterns.

Next are the deposition tools, which add materials to the wafer in controlled layers. These machines deposit metals like copper for wiring, oxides for insulation, and silicon for the transistor structures.

Working alongside them are etching tools, which remove materials to carve out precise patterns. Plasma etchers use high-energy ions, while chemical etchers rely on corrosive substances to achieve this delicate sculpting.

Ion implanters play a key role in the creation of transistors. These machines fire atoms, such as phosphorus or boron, into the silicon wafer to alter its electrical properties and form the P and N regions essential for semiconductor operation. After this bombardment, annealing tools repair the silicon lattice by heating the wafer to restore its structure.

Two other critical categories are cleaning and inspection tools. Cleaning machines use ultra-pure water and chemicals to remove any contaminants that could compromise the wafer, while metrology tools inspect the layers for defects. Scanning electron microscopes and other advanced imaging systems ensure that each step of the process is executed with nanometer-level precision.

Amid this intricate dance of machinery, the silicon wafer serves as the starting point and foundation for all production. These wafers, cut from large cylindrical ingots of purified silicon, are polished to an almost mirror-like finish. Each wafer measures approximately 300 millimeters in diameter and is barely three-quarters of a millimeter thick. On this delicate surface, transistors are built layer by layer in a process requiring extraordinary precision.

The wafer is more than just a physical platform; it is a canvas upon which billions of transistors are intricately arranged. Its uniform crystalline structure provides the stability needed for microchip operation. Before any manufacturing begins, wafers undergo rigorous preparation to ensure their surface is free from imperfections, as even microscopic defects can lead to costly production failures.

Every machine in the fab plays a part in transforming the silicon wafer into a finished product. The result is not just a collection of circuits, but a masterpiece of engineering, where each transistor and wire contributes to the seamless operation of modern technology. The interplay between these machines and the wafer they work upon highlights the extraordinary precision and complexity of semiconductor manufacturing.

Chapter 3: The Anatomy of a Microchip

An integrated circuit is a marvel of modern engineering, an intricately layered structure that transforms electrical signals into meaningful computations. At its core, it is a carefully organized collection of transistors, wires, and insulating materials, all packed into a piece of silicon no larger than a fingernail. The sheer density of components—billions of transistors arranged in precise patterns—defines the power and complexity of the chip.

At the bottom of an integrated circuit lie the transistors, the fundamental building blocks of all logic gates. These tiny devices act as switches, controlling the flow of electrical currents and enabling the binary logic upon which all digital systems are built. A single transistor can turn a current on or off, representing the 1s and 0s of binary code. When grouped together, they form logic gates such as AND, OR, and NOT, which are the basic operations of computation.

Above the transistors are the layers of interconnects, a complex network of metal wires that distribute electrical signals across the chip. These wires, made from materials like copper, are arranged in multiple layers, each separated by insulating materials to prevent short circuits. The interconnects vary in size and function: local interconnects connect nearby transistors, intermediate interconnects link circuits within a single core, and global interconnects transfer data across the entire chip.

The layers of an integrated circuit are stacked with extraordinary precision. Each successive layer is built using advanced manufacturing techniques, ensuring that the alignment between transistors and interconnects is accurate to within a few nanometers. The insulating materials between these layers provide structural support and prevent electrical interference, creating a stable and reliable environment for the chip's operations.

The transistors themselves are feats of engineering. Modern chips often use FinFET transistors, which are three-dimensional structures designed to maximize efficiency and reduce power consumption. These transistors are so small that their dimensions are measured in nanometers, with each one occupying a fraction of the space of a human hair. Despite their size, they are capable of switching on and off billions of times per second, enabling the rapid computations required for modern technology.

The arrangement of transistors and interconnects within an integrated circuit forms what is known as the chip's architecture. This layout is carefully designed to optimize performance, minimize energy consumption, and maximize the use of available space. The result is a device that can perform complex tasks with astonishing speed and efficiency, all within the constraints of its minuscule footprint.

An integrated circuit is not just a collection of components; it is a harmonious interplay of structure and function. From the transistors at its foundation to the maze of interconnects above, every layer contributes to the chip's ability to process, store, and transmit information. This intricate construction underscores the ingenuity and precision that define the modern digital age.

Interconnects are the lifeblood of an integrated circuit, a sprawling maze of metal wires that links billions of transistors into a cohesive and functional system. These wires act as highways, carrying electrical signals between transistors and enabling the logical operations and data transfers that power modern technology. Without interconnects, the individual transistors would remain isolated, incapable of collaborating to perform complex computations.

The interconnects are not a single layer but a network spread across multiple levels within the chip. At the lowest level, local interconnects link transistors within small circuits, facilitating basic logical operations. Intermediate interconnects span larger distances, connecting circuits within a single processing core. At the highest level, global interconnects form the backbone of the chip, transmitting data across different cores and functional blocks. These layers are meticulously organized, with vias—vertical connections—bridging the different levels.

Each layer of interconnects is made of finely etched metal, typically copper or aluminum, chosen for its excellent conductivity. Insulating materials, often silicon dioxide, separate these layers to prevent short circuits and maintain electrical integrity. The insulating layers are as crucial as the wires themselves, ensuring that signals flow cleanly without interference. The entire network is designed to handle immense volumes of data at incredible speeds, with some pathways carrying signals that switch billions of times per second.

The integration of transistors and interconnects transforms the chip into a functional device. Transistors act as the switches, turning currents on and off to represent binary data. Interconnects distribute these signals, allowing the output of one transistor to become the input of another. This connectivity enables the creation of logic gates, which combine to form circuits capable of performing arithmetic, storing memory, or executing instructions.

Consider a processor core as an example. Within the core, transistors handle specific tasks such as addition, multiplication, or decision-making. The interconnects ensure that the output of one operation is seamlessly passed to the next, coordinating millions of simultaneous processes. Even the most basic function, such as multiplying two numbers, requires thousands of transistors and an intricate web of wires working in perfect harmony.

The design of this network is a careful balancing act. Engineers must optimize the layout to minimize resistance, reduce signal delays, and ensure efficient power distribution. At the same time, they must manage the physical constraints of space and heat, as densely packed interconnects can generate significant thermal challenges.

Together, transistors and interconnects form the core of the integrated circuit's functionality. The transistors provide the raw computational power, while the interconnects orchestrate the flow of data, ensuring that every component works together as a unified whole. This interplay is what allows microchips to perform tasks that range from simple calculations to the complex operations driving artificial intelligence, all within the confines of a device small enough to fit in the palm of your hand.

Chapter 4: The Marvel of Miniaturization

The world of microchip manufacturing operates on a scale so small that it almost defies comprehension. Nanometers, the unit of measurement used to define the dimensions of transistors and interconnects, are at the heart of this scale. To put it into perspective, a single nanometer is one-billionth of a meter. For comparison, a human hair is approximately 80,000 to 100,000 nanometers thick, and even the smallest bacteria are several hundred nanometers in size. Working at this microscopic level is not just a technical achievement but a monumental challenge that defines the cutting edge of modern technology.

Nanometers are critical in semiconductor manufacturing because they represent the dimensions of the key components of a microchip. Transistors, the building blocks of all chips, are now so small that their features are often just a few nanometers wide. This miniaturization allows more transistors to be packed onto a single chip, directly influencing the chip's performance, power efficiency, and overall capabilities. The ability to shrink these dimensions over time has been the driving force behind advancements in computing, known as Moore's Law—the observation that the number of transistors on a chip doubles approximately every two years.

The importance of working at the nanometer scale extends beyond increasing the number of transistors. Smaller transistors consume less power and generate less heat, which is crucial for maintaining the efficiency of modern devices. Additionally, shorter distances for electrical signals to travel within the chip lead to faster processing speeds. This combination of speed, efficiency, and density is what enables modern processors to handle complex tasks, such as running artificial intelligence algorithms or processing high-definition video, with remarkable speed and energy efficiency.

However, working at the nanometer scale presents enormous challenges. At such tiny dimensions, the physical properties of materials begin to change. Quantum effects, which are irrelevant at larger scales, become significant, potentially interfering with the predictable behavior of electrical signals. Manufacturing processes must be executed with near-perfect precision, as even a single atomic-scale defect can disrupt the functionality of a transistor or interconnect. Achieving this level of precision requires cutting-edge equipment, such as extreme ultraviolet (EUV) lithography machines, and constant innovation in materials science and engineering.

The scale of nanometers also introduces logistical challenges in design and testing. Engineers must simulate and validate chip layouts to ensure that every transistor and wire functions correctly in its intended role. This level of complexity demands immense computational resources and a deep understanding of physics, chemistry, and electrical engineering.

Despite these challenges, the shift toward ever-smaller scales continues to drive the evolution of technology. Working at the nanometer scale is what makes it possible to fit the power of a supercomputer into a smartphone or create chips that enable breakthroughs in fields as diverse as medicine, aerospace, and artificial intelligence. Nanometers are more than just a unit of measurement—they are the frontier of human innovation, defining the capabilities of the digital age and shaping the future of technology.

To truly grasp the extraordinary smallness of transistors, it helps to compare their dimensions to everyday objects and familiar biological structures. A modern transistor is often just a few nanometers in size, making it nearly incomprehensible to visualize without a frame of reference. Imagine a human hair, typically around 80,000 to 100,000 nanometers in thickness. Now, consider that a single transistor is so small that you could line up thousands of them across the width of that hair.

Dust particles, another familiar size comparison, are colossal in contrast. A particle of dust measures around 2,500 nanometers, meaning a single speck could obscure entire arrays of transistors. Moving into the realm of biology, mitochondria, often referred to as the powerhouses of cells, measure between 500 and 1,000 nanometers. Even at the smaller end of that scale, a mitochondrion is still orders of magnitude larger than a single transistor.

These comparisons illustrate the mind-boggling scale of miniaturization achieved in modern microchip manufacturing. However, working at such a scale comes with formidable challenges. At the nanoscale, the rules of classical physics often give way to quantum effects. These effects can cause unpredictable behavior in materials, such as electrons tunneling through barriers that, at larger scales, would be impenetrable. Designing transistors that operate reliably under such conditions requires a profound understanding of quantum mechanics and the development of materials engineered at the atomic level.

Contamination is another critical challenge. At this scale, even a single particle of dust can destroy an entire wafer, rendering countless transistors unusable. This is why semiconductor fabrication plants enforce such rigorous cleanliness standards, creating controlled environments where airborne particles are virtually eliminated. Despite these precautions, maintaining absolute purity during the manufacturing process remains a constant battle.

Precision is also paramount. The alignment of layers within a chip must be accurate to within fractions of a nanometer. Any misalignment can disrupt the delicate connections between transistors and interconnects, leading to defective chips. Achieving this precision requires advanced lithography techniques, such as extreme ultraviolet (EUV) lithography, which uses incredibly short wavelengths of light to create patterns at the nanometer scale.

Heat management becomes another significant issue as components shrink. The concentration of transistors in a tiny space generates immense amounts of heat, which must be efficiently dissipated to prevent damage or degradation of performance. Engineers continually innovate cooling methods and materials to manage this thermal output while maintaining chip reliability.

Finally, as transistors shrink, the cost of development and manufacturing escalates. Each advance in miniaturization requires massive investments in research, specialized equipment, and new production techniques. The economic challenge of working at the nanoscale is as daunting as the scientific one, making collaboration across industries and disciplines essential for continued progress.

Despite these challenges, the ability to work at the nanoscale has unlocked possibilities that were once the realm of science fiction. The ever-smaller dimensions of transistors are what enable the exponential growth of computing power, making the digital world faster, more efficient, and more connected than ever before. Transistors at the nanoscale are not just feats of engineering; they are the foundation of the modern technological revolution.

Chapter 5: The Step-by-Step Process of IC Manufacturing

The creation of a microchip is an extraordinary journey, a painstakingly detailed process that spans three months and encompasses an astonishing 940 individual steps. Each of these steps is executed with nanometer-level precision, ensuring that billions of transistors and their interconnecting wires are perfectly aligned to form a functional chip. The complexity of this endeavor is nearly impossible to overstate, yet it can be likened to a craft we're all familiar with: baking a cake.

Imagine a cake with 80 layers, each uniquely shaped and precisely positioned. To create such a masterpiece, the recipe demands nearly a thousand individual steps. Each layer must be baked, cut to its specific design, and carefully stacked atop the previous one without a single flaw. Even the slightest deviation—a temperature off by a single degree, a misstep in the cutting process, or an ingredient added a fraction too soon—can ruin the entire cake, rendering it unsalvageable. Now, scale this process down to a level where each "layer" is measured in nanometers, and you begin to understand the intricate ballet of microchip manufacturing.

The "ingredients" for this microchip cake are no less exotic than the process itself. Materials such as silicon, copper, and tantalum, along with light-sensitive chemicals, are used in exacting quantities to build each layer. These materials are deposited, patterned, etched, and polished with a level of care that rivals the precision of watchmaking, multiplied by the complexity of billions.

Each layer serves a specific purpose in the chip's functionality. Some layers house the transistors that act as switches, while others are composed of insulating materials to separate the circuitry. Additional layers form the interconnects, the intricate maze of wires that bind the transistors into a cohesive network. Together, these layers build the chip's architecture, transforming the flat silicon wafer into a three-dimensional marvel of engineering.

Much like a baker meticulously following a recipe, semiconductor engineers rely on exacting protocols to ensure that each step is executed perfectly. For instance, when applying a photoresist layer to the wafer, the thickness must be uniform down to the nanometer, and the pattern etched into it must align precisely with the layers below. This level of precision is repeated across all 940 steps, with frequent cleaning and inspection stages interwoven to catch any potential defects before they compromise the entire chip.

The analogy of a cake simplifies the daunting complexity of microchip manufacturing, but the reality is even more demanding. Each layer of this "cake" represents months, if not years, of research and development. The tools required to craft these layers are among the most advanced machines in the world, and the entire process must be carried out in an environment where even a single speck of dust could spell disaster.

By the time the final layer is placed and the wafer is ready for testing, the "cake" is not just complete—it is a masterpiece of technology. Each microchip, born of this arduous process, embodies the pinnacle of human ingenuity and precision, capable of powering the digital age in ways that continue to redefine what is possible.

The process of crafting a microchip unfolds through a meticulously orchestrated series of steps, each building upon the last to create the intricate structures and connections necessary for its functionality. At the heart of this process are several core manufacturing steps that are repeated countless times, layering materials with atomic-level precision until the final chip takes form. These steps include depositing silicon dioxide, applying photoresist and patterning with

UV light, etching and depositing materials, and planarizing the surface to prepare for the next layer.

The journey begins with the deposition of silicon dioxide, a critical insulating material. Using a method known as chemical vapor deposition, a thin layer of silicon dioxide is applied uniformly across the surface of the silicon wafer. This layer serves as the foundation for subsequent patterns and provides electrical insulation between the various layers of the chip. The uniformity and purity of this layer are essential, as even the smallest inconsistencies can disrupt the intricate circuits that will be built upon it.

Next, a light-sensitive material known as photoresist is applied to the wafer. This material is spread evenly using a process called spin coating, which ensures a thin, uniform layer. The wafer is then exposed to ultraviolet (UV) light through a stencil-like mask called a photomask. This mask contains the blueprint for the specific pattern to be imprinted on the photoresist. Where the UV light strikes the photoresist, it weakens the material, allowing the exposed areas to be removed during a subsequent development step. This leaves behind a precise pattern on the wafer, which serves as a guide for the next stages.

With the patterned photoresist in place, the wafer moves on to the etching process. Etching removes the exposed silicon dioxide or other materials beneath the photoresist, carving out the intended design. This step can be performed using either chemical etchants or plasma-based techniques, depending on the material and the desired precision. Once the etching is complete, the remaining photoresist is stripped away, leaving a clean, patterned surface ready for the addition of new materials.

Deposition follows, adding conductive or insulating materials into the etched areas. For example, metals like copper are deposited to form the interconnects, the pathways that link transistors and other components. These depositions must fill the etched patterns precisely, ensuring complete coverage without overfilling.

After deposition, the wafer undergoes planarization, a process that smooths and flattens the surface to prepare for the next layer. This is achieved through chemical-mechanical planarization (CMP), which combines abrasive pads and chemical slurries to polish the wafer. Planarization is critical to maintaining alignment between layers; any unevenness could cause misalignments in the subsequent patterns, rendering the chip defective.

These core steps—depositing, patterning, etching, and planarization—are repeated in cycles, each building a new layer of the microchip. Each cycle adds complexity to the chip's structure, stacking transistors, interconnects, and insulating materials in a precise sequence. Over time, these layers form the intricate three-dimensional architecture of the chip, culminating in a functional integrated circuit capable of powering modern technology.

The repetition of these cycles, each executed with nanometer-level precision, highlights the extraordinary complexity of microchip manufacturing. Through hundreds of iterations, the silicon wafer is transformed from a blank slate into a dense, multi-layered network of transistors and wires, a testament to the sophistication and ingenuity of semiconductor engineering.

Chapter 6: Tools of Precision

The creation of microchips relies on a suite of highly specialized tools, each tailored to execute a specific phase of the manufacturing process. These tools fall into distinct categories, working in harmony to transform a simple silicon wafer into an intricate integrated circuit. From patterning the blueprint to ensuring defect-free layers, each tool plays an indispensable role in the fabrication process.

The first category, mask-making tools, includes the photolithography systems that define the chip's intricate patterns. These tools project ultraviolet light through a photomask, imprinting a precise design onto a light-sensitive photoresist layer applied to the wafer. The photomask itself acts as a stencil, dictating where the UV light can pass and creating the detailed patterns required for billions of transistors and interconnects. Supporting tools such as spin coaters, which evenly apply the photoresist, and photoresist developers, which remove the exposed areas, are also critical in this phase.

Deposition machines form the second category, responsible for adding layers of materials to the wafer. These machines deposit various substances, including silicon dioxide for insulation, metals like copper for interconnects, and crystalline silicon for transistors. The deposition processes vary based on the material being applied, with techniques like chemical vapor deposition (CVD), physical vapor deposition (PVD), and atomic layer deposition (ALD) offering precise control over thickness and composition. Each material forms a key part of the chip's structure, and the deposition must be flawless to ensure the chip's performance and reliability.

Etching systems come next, tasked with removing unwanted material to sculpt the wafer's layers into their final form. These systems use either chemical etchants or high-energy plasma to carve out precise patterns defined by the photolithography process. Plasma etchers, for example, rely on ionized gases to react with and remove specific regions of the wafer's surface. The etched patterns create spaces for interconnects or define the boundaries of transistors, shaping the wafer layer by layer.

Ion implantation machines are a specialized category, essential for creating the transistors that power the chip. These tools fire ions, such as phosphorus or boron, into the silicon wafer at high velocities, embedding them deep within the material to alter its electrical properties. This process defines the P-type and N-type regions that enable transistors to switch electrical signals. Following ion implantation, annealing tools are used to repair any damage to the silicon lattice caused by the high-energy bombardment.

Cleaning tools are another vital component of the fab. At the nanometer scale, even the smallest particle of dust or residue can render an entire wafer unusable. Cleaning systems use ultra-pure water, chemicals, and techniques like nitrogen drying to remove contaminants at every stage of production. These tools are used frequently throughout the manufacturing process to ensure pristine conditions, maintaining the wafer's integrity as layers are added and shaped.

The final category includes metrology and inspection tools, which ensure the wafer's layers meet exacting standards. These tools include scanning electron microscopes (SEMs) and other advanced imaging systems capable of nanometer-level resolution. They inspect the wafer for defects, confirm alignment between layers, and measure the thickness and uniformity of deposited materials. Metrology tools provide critical feedback, allowing engineers to identify and correct issues before they propagate through subsequent steps.

Together, these categories of semiconductor tools form the backbone of the microchip manufacturing process. Each tool is a marvel of engineering, designed to execute its task with extraordinary precision. The collaboration between these machines transforms raw silicon into the dense, multi-layered structures that power the modern digital world, a testament to the ingenuity and sophistication of semiconductor technology.

Photolithography is the cornerstone of microchip manufacturing, the process that enables the creation of the intricate patterns required to form billions of transistors and interconnects on a silicon wafer. Often referred to as the heart of integrated circuit (IC) patterning, photolithography translates the chip's design into physical reality with nanometer-level precision, making it one of the most critical and complex steps in semiconductor fabrication.

At its core, photolithography is a process of projecting a pattern onto a light-sensitive material called photoresist, which is applied as a thin layer across the wafer. The pattern originates from a photomask, a stencil-like sheet that contains the design for a single layer of the chip. The photomask is positioned between a powerful ultraviolet (UV) light source and the wafer, allowing light to pass through its transparent regions while blocking it in others. The UV light interacts with the photoresist, chemically altering the areas exposed to the light.

The photolithography process begins with the preparation of the wafer. First, a spin coater spreads the photoresist evenly across its surface. This step is followed by a soft bake, where the wafer is gently heated to remove solvents from the photoresist, ensuring its stability during exposure. Once prepared, the wafer moves to the photolithography tool, a machine equipped with an intense UV light source, an optical system, and a wafer stage.

Inside the photolithography tool, the UV light is focused and directed through the photomask. Advanced optics, including lenses and mirrors, shrink the pattern from the photomask to a fraction of its original size, enabling the creation of features measured in nanometers. The wafer stage moves in precise steps, allowing the pattern to be repeated across the entire wafer, forming identical layouts for hundreds of microchips.

After exposure, the wafer undergoes a development step, where chemicals wash away the photoresist in areas exposed to the UV light. This leaves behind a patterned layer of photoresist, which serves as a protective mask during subsequent etching or deposition processes. The pattern carved into the photoresist defines where materials will be added or removed in later steps.

The precision of photolithography is nothing short of astonishing. Modern tools, like those using extreme ultraviolet (EUV) lithography, achieve feature sizes as small as a few nanometers. This level of detail is necessary to meet the demands of today's microchips, which pack billions of transistors onto a single wafer. The success of this process depends on the alignment between the photomask and the wafer, requiring sub-nanometer accuracy to ensure each layer matches perfectly with those below it.

Photolithography is not without its challenges. The shorter the wavelength of light, the finer the details that can be achieved, but working with shorter wavelengths requires increasingly sophisticated equipment and materials. The cost of photolithography tools is staggering, with some machines exceeding $150 million each, reflecting the immense technological advancements they embody.

Despite its complexity and cost, photolithography remains indispensable to semiconductor manufacturing. It is the enabler of miniaturization, allowing microchips to grow more powerful and efficient with each generation. Every pattern etched onto a wafer during this process represents a step closer to creating the integrated circuits that power the digital world, making photolithography a cornerstone of modern technology.

Chapter 7: The Birth of a Transistor

Creating transistors, the essential building blocks of microchips, involves precise processes that manipulate silicon at the atomic level. Two critical steps in this transformation are **ion implantation** and **annealing**, which work in tandem to form the electrical properties that make transistors functional. These steps are pivotal in defining the P-type and N-type regions of the silicon wafer, enabling the switching mechanisms that underlie all digital logic.

Ion Implantation: Embedding Electrical Properties

Ion implantation is a process where high-energy ions, such as phosphorus or boron, are accelerated and directed into the silicon wafer. These ions act as dopants, altering the electrical conductivity of specific regions within the silicon. Phosphorus, a donor atom, adds free electrons to create N-type silicon, while boron, an acceptor atom, creates P-type silicon by introducing holes (the absence of electrons). Together, these regions form the foundation for transistors, enabling them to control electrical currents effectively.

The process begins by preparing the wafer with a patterned photoresist layer that acts as a mask, protecting certain areas while leaving others exposed. The ion implanter, a machine resembling a miniature particle accelerator, generates a beam of ions and directs it toward the exposed regions of the silicon. The ions penetrate the wafer to precise depths, determined by their energy and the angle of implantation. The control over depth and concentration ensures that the doped regions meet the specific requirements for the chip's design.

Ion implantation is an incredibly precise process, but the high-energy collisions between ions and the silicon lattice can damage its crystalline structure. This damage creates disruptions that must be repaired for the silicon to regain its desired properties.

Annealing: Repairing and Activating the Silicon

Annealing is the next step, where the wafer is heated to high temperatures to restore its crystalline structure and activate the dopants. This thermal process allows the silicon atoms to rearrange themselves, healing the damage caused by ion implantation. At the same time, the heat helps the dopant atoms integrate seamlessly into the silicon lattice, ensuring they are in the correct positions to modify the material's electrical properties effectively.

The annealing process is performed using specialized equipment that rapidly heats and cools the wafer, ensuring precise temperature control. In some cases, lasers are used for localized annealing, targeting specific regions without affecting the rest of the wafer. This method is particularly useful for advanced chips, where extreme precision is required.

By the end of the annealing step, the silicon wafer has well-defined P-type and N-type regions, creating the essential components of transistors. These regions form the junctions that allow transistors to act as switches, controlling the flow of electrical current in response to input signals. This switching capability is the foundation of all digital logic, enabling the binary operations that power modern computing.

The Role of Ion Implantation and Annealing in the Big Picture

Together, ion implantation and annealing are foundational to microchip manufacturing, laying the groundwork for the transistors that drive digital systems. These processes must be executed with nanometer-level precision, as the performance of the entire chip depends on the accuracy and quality of the doped regions. The ability to precisely control electrical properties at such a small scale is a testament to the advanced science and engineering behind modern semiconductor fabrication.

These steps are repeated billions of times across the wafer, forming the vast array of transistors that make up an integrated circuit. Each transistor is a tiny switch, capable of turning electrical currents on or off, and collectively, they create the logic gates, memory cells, and processing units that define a chip's functionality. Ion implantation and annealing may be just two steps in the complex process of microchip manufacturing, but they are indispensable in bringing transistors—and the digital age itself—to life.

Microchip manufacturing is a highly structured process, divided into two major phases: front-end and back-end processes. Each phase plays a crucial role in transforming a silicon wafer into a functional chip. The front-end focuses on building the intricate structures of transistors and interconnects, while the back-end ensures these chips are tested, packaged, and prepared for integration into devices.

Front-End Processes: Building the Core of the Chip

The front-end processes occur within the cleanroom of a semiconductor fabrication plant. This phase is where the silicon wafer is transformed into a dense network of transistors and interconnects through hundreds of meticulous steps. Key operations like ion implantation, photolithography, deposition, etching, and annealing take place here. Each layer of the chip is built sequentially, with nanometer-level precision, to form the three-dimensional architecture of the integrated circuit.

The creation of transistors is a highlight of the front-end process. These tiny switches are crafted using techniques such as ion implantation to define the P and N regions and annealing to activate and repair the silicon lattice. The interconnects, composed of layers of metal wires, are added later to link these transistors into a cohesive network capable of executing complex computations. The front-end is all about precision and purity, as even the smallest imperfection can compromise the functionality of the final chip.

Back-End Processes: Testing and Packaging

Once the front-end processes are complete, the wafer moves to the back-end phase. Here, the focus shifts from building to preparing the chip for practical use. The first step involves testing the individual chips on the wafer to ensure they function as intended. Advanced tools probe each chip to identify defects or areas of reduced performance. This process is critical for categorizing the chips based on their capabilities, a step known as binning.

Defective or semi-functional chips are not wasted but are instead categorized for use in lower-performance products. For example, a chip with partially functioning cores might be marketed as a less powerful processor. Once the functional chips are identified, the wafer is cut into individual units using lasers or precision saws.

Each chip is then mounted onto a substrate, often called an interposer, which serves as a bridge to the larger printed circuit board. Additional components, such as protective covers and heat spreaders, are added to ensure durability and efficient thermal management. The final step in the back-end process is packaging, where the chip is enclosed and labeled for sale and integration into electronic devices.

The Role of P and N Regions in Transistor Operation

At the heart of a transistor's functionality are the P and N regions, which are critical to its ability to act as a switch for electrical signals. These regions are created during the front-end processes through ion implantation, where dopant atoms like boron (for P-type) and phosphorus (for N-type) are embedded into the silicon lattice.

In a basic field-effect transistor (FET), these regions form the source and drain terminals, while the gate, positioned between them, controls the flow of current. When a voltage is applied to the gate, it creates an electric field that either allows or blocks the movement of charge carriers (electrons or holes) between the source and drain. In N-type regions, the carriers are electrons, while in P-type regions, they are holes, which are effectively the absence of electrons.

The precise placement and properties of the P and N regions are what enable transistors to switch on and off with incredible speed. This switching mechanism forms the foundation of binary logic, the language of all digital systems. Whether powering a simple calculator or a complex supercomputer, every operation boils down to the controlled flow of electrons within these tiny regions.

Connecting the Two Phases

The success of the back-end phase depends entirely

on the precision of the front-end processes. The creation of functional P and N regions, the meticulous layering of transistors and interconnects, and the overall integrity of the chip's architecture determine how well the chip will perform in its final form. Together, these phases form a seamless pipeline, transforming raw silicon into a polished product ready to power the devices of the digital age.

Chapter 8: Testing and Assembly

After the complex and meticulous front-end processes are complete, the silicon wafer moves into a critical stage of its journey: testing. Each wafer, now covered with hundreds or even thousands of microchips, undergoes rigorous evaluations to determine the functionality of every individual chip. This stage ensures that only the operational chips proceed to packaging and assembly.

Advanced testing equipment is used to probe each chip on the wafer. A set of fine needles or electronic probes touches down on designated contact points of the chips to apply electrical signals and measure their responses. These tests verify whether the transistors switch correctly, the interconnects transmit signals without interruption, and the overall architecture performs as designed. The results provide a clear picture of each chip's capabilities, allowing engineers to identify fully functional chips as well as those with partial or complete defects.

Defects can arise from a variety of sources, such as contaminants during the manufacturing process, misalignments in the photolithography patterns, or inconsistencies in material deposition. Given the scale of the features being measured—down to nanometers—these imperfections are inevitable to some extent, making the testing phase essential for ensuring the quality and reliability of the final product.

Once testing is complete, the process of categorization begins. Chips are sorted into different performance tiers based on the results of the tests. This categorization is known as binning and reflects the diverse functional outcomes of the manufacturing process. Fully functional chips, with all cores and components operating at their intended performance levels, are placed into the highest performance categories. These chips are typically sold as flagship models, offering the most advanced capabilities.

However, not all chips perform perfectly. Some may have partially functioning cores or minor defects that do not compromise their overall usability. These chips are binned into lower performance tiers and marketed as less powerful or more budget-friendly versions. For instance, a chip with one or two defective cores might still be sold as a mid-range processor, while chips with non-functioning integrated graphics may be categorized into product lines that do not require graphical capabilities.

Binning is an effective strategy that maximizes the utility of each wafer, reducing waste while creating a range of products for different market segments. By identifying and categorizing chips based on their functionality, manufacturers can offer a variety of options to meet the diverse needs of consumers and industries. This process not only ensures the efficiency of the production pipeline but also highlights the adaptability of modern semiconductor manufacturing, where even imperfections are harnessed to create value.

Once the wafer testing and binning processes are complete, the journey of transforming raw silicon into usable microchips continues with the steps of cutting, flipping, and assembling the chips. The circular silicon wafer, now marked with functional and categorized chips, is carefully sliced into individual units. This cutting process, often performed using high-precision lasers or diamond saws, ensures that each chip is separated cleanly and with minimal damage to the delicate circuitry.

After cutting, each chip—referred to as a die—undergoes flipping. This step is essential because the active side of the chip, containing the intricate network of transistors and interconnects, must face downward to connect with the substrate. The substrate, often referred to as the interposer, acts as a bridge between the die and the printed circuit board (PCB). It distributes the connection points from the densely packed die to a larger, more accessible grid that can interface with other components in a device.

The assembly process involves carefully positioning the flipped die onto the substrate, ensuring precise alignment of the contact points. Once in place, the die is securely attached using advanced bonding techniques, such as solder bumps or conductive adhesives. This assembly is a critical step, as it establishes the electrical pathways that allow the chip to communicate with the rest of a device.

To ensure the durability and performance of the chip, additional components are added. One of the most important is the heat spreader, a metal plate designed to dissipate the heat generated by the chip during operation. Modern microchips, especially those used in high-performance applications, produce significant heat due to the density and speed of their transistors. The heat spreader protects the chip from thermal damage by evenly distributing the heat across its surface, allowing it to be efficiently carried away by external cooling systems.

The final stage of this process is packaging. The assembled chip, now equipped with a heat spreader, is encased in a protective housing. This package not only shields the delicate internal components from physical damage and environmental factors such as moisture and dust but also provides the interface through which the chip connects to a device's motherboard. Packaging involves careful placement of pins, pads, or other connectors that align with the landing grid array on a PCB.

Each packaged chip undergoes a final round of testing to confirm its performance and reliability. Once verified, the chips are labeled, sorted, and prepared for shipment to manufacturers, where they will be integrated into a wide range of products, from smartphones and computers to cars and medical devices. This phase completes the transformation of raw silicon into a fully functional, market-ready microchip, ready to power the technologies that define modern life.

Chapter 9: Challenges in Microchip Manufacturing

Microchip manufacturing is a process defined by its extraordinary demands for precision. At the heart of this need lies the nanometer scale, where the smallest features of a chip—such as transistors and interconnects—are measured in billionths of a meter. Each transistor is often just a few nanometers in size, with billions of these tiny structures packed onto a single chip. Achieving this level of density requires manufacturing techniques that operate with a precision unimaginable in most other industries.

Nanometer-level precision is not simply a goal but an absolute necessity. Even a minor misalignment of a few nanometers during the layering process can disrupt the connections between transistors, rendering an entire chip defective. Similarly, variations in material thickness, inconsistencies in etching, or improper deposition can lead to performance issues or outright failure. The demand for this precision intensifies with each new generation of chips, as manufacturers strive to make components smaller, faster, and more energy-efficient.

One of the greatest challenges to achieving this precision is the ever-present risk of contaminants and defects. At the nanometer scale, even a single particle of dust, invisible to the naked eye, can cause catastrophic damage. A contaminant particle can block light during the photolithography process, create irregularities during deposition, or interfere with electrical pathways, compromising the chip's functionality.

Defects can also arise from within the manufacturing process itself. Imperfections in the silicon wafer, misaligned photomasks, or errors during ion implantation are all potential sources of failure. As chips become more complex, with billions of transistors operating in unison, the probability of a defect affecting performance increases significantly.

To mitigate these risks, semiconductor fabrication plants implement rigorous strategies. The cleanroom environment is one of the most effective defenses against contaminants. Air in the cleanroom is filtered continuously, maintaining a purity level thousands of times greater than that of a hospital operating room. Workers wear full-body suits, known as "bunny suits," to prevent particles from their skin, hair, or breath from entering the controlled environment. Even vibrations and temperature fluctuations are minimized to preserve the integrity of the manufacturing process.

Advanced inspection and cleaning tools are employed at every stage of production to identify and remove potential contaminants. Metrology systems, capable of nanometer-level resolution, continuously monitor the wafer for defects, ensuring that errors are caught early and corrected before they propagate through the manufacturing process. Cleaning systems use ultra-pure water and specialized chemicals to remove even the smallest residues from the wafer's surface.

In addition to these physical measures, manufacturers rely on sophisticated design and simulation software to anticipate and address potential challenges. These tools help engineers optimize chip layouts, predict material behavior, and ensure that each step of the process adheres to exacting specifications. Automated systems and robotics further reduce the risk of human error, enhancing the precision and reliability of each operation.

Despite these precautions, some level of defects is inevitable. This is why rigorous testing and binning processes are integral to microchip production. Functional chips are separated from defective ones, and semi-functional chips are repurposed for lower-performance applications. This approach minimizes waste and ensures that the maximum number of usable chips is extracted from each wafer.

Nanometer-level precision and the management of contaminants and defects are fundamental to the success of modern semiconductor manufacturing. These efforts are what make it possible to produce the high-performance, reliable microchips that power today's technology, driving the innovation that defines the digital age.

The production of microchips is among the most resource-intensive and costly undertakings in modern manufacturing. Semiconductor fabrication plants, or fabs, represent multi-billion-dollar investments, with cutting-edge facilities often exceeding $10 billion in construction and equipment costs. The extraordinary expense is a reflection of the complexity, precision, and advanced technology required to produce chips at the nanometer scale.

One major factor contributing to the high cost is the specialized equipment used in fabs. Each machine, from deposition tools to photolithography systems, is designed to perform a specific task with nanometer-level precision. A single photolithography machine, particularly those utilizing extreme ultraviolet (EUV) technology, can cost over $150 million. Fabs require hundreds of such machines, each tailored to execute a specific phase of the 940-step manufacturing process. The cost of maintenance, calibration, and upgrading these machines adds further to the expense.

Beyond the machinery, the environment itself is a significant investment. The cleanroom, where wafers are processed, must maintain air purity levels far superior to any other industry. This requires advanced filtration systems, temperature and humidity control, and vibration-dampening measures, all of which add to the operational costs. Additionally, the materials used in chip production—ultra-pure silicon, specialized chemicals, and rare metals like tantalum—are costly and must meet stringent quality standards.

Time is another critical factor. Each wafer takes approximately three months to complete, moving through hundreds of meticulously orchestrated steps. This extended production timeline demands substantial human and financial resources, with thousands of skilled workers, engineers, and scientists required to oversee the process. Even minor errors can lead to significant financial losses, as a single defective wafer can represent tens of thousands of dollars in wasted materials and labor.

Protecting intellectual property (IP) in this fiercely competitive industry adds another layer of complexity and cost. The design and manufacturing processes of microchips are the culmination of years of research and billions of dollars in development. These innovations represent a company's most valuable assets, making them prime targets for industrial espionage, counterfeiting, and reverse engineering.

To safeguard their IP, semiconductor companies implement robust security measures. Fabs operate with strict access controls, ensuring that only authorized personnel can enter sensitive areas. Data encryption, surveillance systems, and cyber defenses are standard, protecting digital blueprints and operational details from theft. Additionally, companies often patent their designs and manufacturing techniques, creating legal barriers against competitors attempting to replicate their technology.

Despite these efforts, the risk of IP theft remains high. In a global industry where production often involves collaboration across borders, ensuring that proprietary information is protected at every stage of the supply chain is an ongoing challenge. Partnerships with third-party manufacturers, or foundries, require careful negotiation to maintain control over proprietary processes while benefiting from the foundry's expertise and scale.

The combination of astronomical costs and the constant need to protect valuable IP underscores why fabs are not only expensive but also pivotal to a company's success. They are not merely factories but centers of innovation, housing the technology and expertise that drive the digital age. The stakes are enormous, as the chips produced in these facilities power everything from consumer electronics to critical infrastructure, making the investments and safeguards essential to maintaining a competitive edge in a rapidly evolving industry.

Chapter 10: The Economics of Silicon

The transformation of a simple $100 silicon wafer into a $100,000 collection of microchips is a journey that encapsulates the pinnacle of modern technology, precision engineering, and scientific innovation. This remarkable escalation in value reflects the immense effort, expertise, and resources required to create some of the most complex devices in existence.

The journey begins with raw quartzite, refined into ultra-pure silicon and formed into large cylindrical ingots. These ingots are sliced into thin, mirror-like wafers, each costing around $100. At this stage, the wafer is simply a blank slate—a circular sheet of silicon with no inherent functionality. Its potential value lies entirely in the manufacturing processes it will undergo.

The first step in adding value to the wafer is its entry into the cleanroom environment of a semiconductor fabrication plant. Over the course of three months, the wafer is meticulously processed through approximately 940 steps, each adding layers of transistors, interconnects, and insulating materials. The cost of this transformation is driven by the extraordinary precision required at the nanometer scale and the advanced machinery involved. A single photolithography machine, essential for patterning the wafer, can cost over $150 million, and fabs require hundreds of such tools, each contributing to the chip's ultimate value.

As the wafer moves from tool to tool, intricate patterns are etched and deposited onto its surface, creating the dense networks of transistors and wires that define its functionality. Each layer represents a combination of cutting-edge science and exacting craftsmanship, ensuring that the components align perfectly. By the time this process is complete, the wafer is populated with hundreds or even thousands of individual chips, each containing billions of transistors. This is where the wafer's value begins to multiply.

Once the front-end processes are finished, the wafer undergoes rigorous testing to identify functional chips. This stage is critical, as even minor defects can render a chip unusable. The functional chips are categorized and binned based on their performance, with the highest-performing chips destined for premium applications. These chips alone significantly boost the wafer's value, as high-performance processors are in demand for devices like servers, gaming systems, and advanced AI applications.

The journey continues in the back-end phase, where the wafer is cut into individual dies. Each die is flipped, assembled onto a substrate, and equipped with a heat spreader for thermal management. This assembly process enhances the chip's durability and prepares it for integration into devices. The addition of packaging—an enclosure that provides protection and connectivity—further increases the chip's value, making it ready for distribution to manufacturers.

By the time the process is complete, the original $100 wafer has undergone a transformation that reflects not just its physical components but the expertise, technology, and effort invested in its creation. A single high-performance chip from that wafer might sell for hundreds or even thousands of dollars, and with hundreds of chips on a single wafer, the total value can easily exceed $100,000. This dramatic increase is a testament to the complexity and precision of semiconductor manufacturing, where each step adds layers of functionality, reliability, and market value.

The journey of a silicon wafer from a raw material to a $100,000 treasure is a microcosm of the digital age. It represents the incredible advances in technology that have made it possible to turn something as simple as silicon into the driving force behind the devices and systems that power our world. This transformation not only highlights the economic significance of semiconductor manufacturing but also underscores the ingenuity and collaboration required to achieve such extraordinary outcomes.

Microchips, despite their diminutive size, are among the most valuable items in the modern world. When compared to precious metals like gold and platinum, the economic worth of microchips often far surpasses their weight in these materials. A fully populated silicon wafer, which starts as a $100 raw material, can easily reach a value of $100,000 or more once transformed into functional chips. This makes microchips roughly ten times more valuable than gold by weight. However, their value is not derived from rarity but from the immense engineering and technological innovation that goes into their creation.

Unlike gold, which is valuable for its intrinsic properties, microchips owe their worth to their function as the backbone of modern technology.

They power everything from smartphones and laptops to vehicles and medical equipment. The functionality embedded in each microchip far outweighs its physical composition, making these devices indispensable in a world driven by data and connectivity. A single high-performance processor can deliver capabilities that are vital for industries ranging from healthcare and telecommunications to defense and entertainment.

This extraordinary value is made possible by a global semiconductor supply chain that is as intricate and interconnected as the chips themselves. The journey of a microchip from raw materials to finished product involves contributions from multiple countries, each specializing in specific aspects of the production process. This interdependence reflects the complexity and scale of the semiconductor industry.

The supply chain begins with raw materials such as silicon, copper, and rare earth elements, which are extracted and refined in resource-rich regions like

China, Russia, and Australia. These materials are then transported to facilities specializing in the production of silicon wafers, primarily located in countries like Japan, South Korea, and Taiwan. These wafers serve as the foundation for the microchip manufacturing process.

The fabrication of chips takes place in semiconductor fabs, concentrated in technology hubs like Taiwan, South Korea, and the United States. Taiwan's TSMC and South Korea's Samsung dominate this stage, producing chips for industries worldwide. These fabs rely on equipment from countries like the Netherlands, where ASML produces the world's only extreme ultraviolet (EUV) lithography machines, and the United States and Japan, which supply other essential tools and chemicals.

Once the chips are fabricated, they are tested, packaged, and assembled in specialized facilities, often located in Southeast Asia, including Malaysia and the Philippines. These facilities prepare the chips for integration into products like smartphones, laptops, and vehicles. The finished products are then distributed globally, completing the cycle that began with raw materials.

The semiconductor supply chain's global nature is both a strength and a vulnerability. It allows companies to leverage the expertise and resources of different regions, ensuring efficiency and innovation. However, it also means that disruptions in one part of the chain—whether due to natural disasters, geopolitical tensions, or pandemics—can ripple across the entire industry. Recent chip shortages have highlighted the critical need for resilience and collaboration within this system.

The combined value of microchips and the intricacy of the global supply chain underscore the immense importance of semiconductors in the modern world. They are not just components but the foundation of a digital ecosystem that drives economic growth, technological innovation, and societal advancement. As demand for advanced technology continues to grow, the value of microchips and the interdependence of their supply chain will only become more pronounced.

Chapter 11: The Future of Microchips

As semiconductor manufacturing advances, the demand for smaller, faster, and more efficient transistors drives the development of cutting-edge technologies like FinFETs and other next-generation designs. Traditional planar transistors, which have served the industry for decades, have reached physical limitations in terms of size and power efficiency. FinFETs, or Fin Field-Effect Transistors, represent a transformative shift, offering significant improvements in performance and energy consumption by introducing a three-dimensional structure.

FinFETs are named for their distinctive "fin-like" structure, which rises vertically from the silicon substrate. Unlike planar transistors, where the gate controls current flow across a flat surface, FinFETs surround the channel on three sides, providing better electrostatic control. This design reduces leakage currents, allowing FinFETs to operate more efficiently at smaller scales. Their ability to pack more functionality into a smaller footprint makes them ideal for modern chips, enabling billions of transistors to function reliably on a single die.

The industry is now looking beyond FinFETs toward even more advanced technologies, such as gate-all-around (GAA) transistors. GAA designs take the FinFET concept further by enclosing the channel entirely with the gate, offering even greater control over current flow. These innovations are critical for achieving continued miniaturization while addressing the challenges of power density and heat generation.

The adoption of such next-generation transistors is bolstered by the increasing role of artificial intelligence (AI) and automation within semiconductor fabrication plants. The complexity of modern chip designs, combined with the precision required for nanometer-level manufacturing, makes manual oversight insufficient. AI-driven systems and automation technologies have become essential for optimizing every aspect of the production process, from design validation to defect detection.

AI enhances the efficiency of fabs by analyzing vast amounts of data generated during manufacturing. Machine learning algorithms can predict equipment performance, identify potential failures, and optimize tool parameters in real-time, reducing downtime and improving yield rates. Automated systems handle tasks like wafer handling, material deposition, and pattern alignment with nanometer precision, ensuring consistency across thousands of steps.

One of the most transformative applications of AI in fabs is in defect detection. Traditional inspection methods rely on manual or rule-based approaches that may overlook subtle anomalies. AI-powered inspection systems, however, can identify patterns that indicate potential defects, even at scales imperceptible to the human eye. These systems not only improve quality control but also provide valuable insights for continuous process improvement.

Automation extends to the logistics of wafer movement within the fab. Overhead transport systems, guided by AI, ensure that wafers are delivered to the right tools at the right time, minimizing bottlenecks and maximizing throughput. The integration of robotics further enhances precision and efficiency, reducing the risk of human error in handling delicate wafers.

The combination of emerging transistor technologies like FinFETs and the integration of AI and automation in fabs represents a new era in semiconductor manufacturing. Together, they enable the production of chips that are not only more powerful and efficient but also manufactured with unprecedented accuracy and speed. These innovations are driving the industry forward, ensuring that it can meet the growing demands of a technology-driven world.

As semiconductor manufacturing continues to push the boundaries of miniaturization, sustainability and scalability have emerged as critical challenges. Shrinking transistors to ever-smaller dimensions, while maintaining performance and efficiency, requires immense resources, innovative materials, and groundbreaking engineering. However, these advancements come with environmental, technical, and economic hurdles that the industry must address to ensure a sustainable future.

The environmental impact of chip manufacturing is significant. Semiconductor fabs consume enormous amounts of energy and water to maintain cleanroom environments and power the intricate processes of wafer production. The chemicals used in etching, deposition, and cleaning can generate hazardous waste, requiring meticulous management to prevent environmental harm. As the demand for microchips grows, driven by trends like artificial intelligence, 5G, and IoT, the industry faces pressure to reduce its ecological footprint while scaling up production.

To meet these challenges, companies are investing in sustainable practices, such as using renewable energy to power fabs and implementing advanced recycling systems for water and chemicals. Innovations in materials science also hold promise, with researchers exploring alternatives to conventional silicon that require less energy-intensive processing. Additionally, improving process efficiency through AI and automation not only boosts yield rates but also minimizes waste, contributing to a more sustainable production pipeline.

On the technical front, scaling down transistor dimensions has reached physical limits that challenge the traditional methods of miniaturization. At dimensions below five nanometers, quantum effects like electron tunneling and increased resistance in interconnects become more pronounced, threatening the reliability and efficiency of chips. These barriers have prompted the exploration of alternative architectures, such as three-dimensional chip stacking, which increases computational density without further shrinking individual transistors.

Looking ahead, the coming decades are expected to bring transformative advancements in microchip technology. Emerging materials, such as graphene and transition metal dichalcogenides, offer properties that could revolutionize transistor design. These materials enable faster electron mobility and better thermal conductivity, paving the way for devices that operate with greater speed and efficiency.

Quantum computing is another frontier poised to redefine the semiconductor industry. While still in its early stages, quantum processors promise unparalleled computational power by leveraging the principles of quantum mechanics. Unlike traditional chips that rely on binary logic, quantum chips use qubits, which can represent multiple states simultaneously, opening new possibilities for solving complex problems.

Artificial intelligence and machine learning will also play a central role in shaping the future of microchips. AI-driven design tools are already accelerating the development of new architectures by simulating and optimizing layouts with unprecedented precision. As AI systems become more sophisticated, they will likely enable breakthroughs in materials discovery, manufacturing processes, and chip functionality.

The integration of chips into every facet of life will continue to expand. From autonomous vehicles and smart cities to personalized healthcare and space exploration, microchips will be at the core of technological progress. Advances in edge computing and energy-efficient processors will ensure that devices can perform complex tasks locally, reducing the need for centralized data processing and enabling faster, more reliable interactions.

Despite the challenges of sustainability and scaling, the semiconductor industry remains a beacon of innovation. By embracing new materials, architectures, and methodologies, it will not only overcome current limitations but also unlock possibilities that redefine the relationship between technology and humanity. The coming decades promise an era where microchips are not only more powerful and efficient but also integral to a sustainable and interconnected world.

Conclusion

The journey of microchip manufacturing is a testament to human ingenuity and the relentless pursuit of precision. From the humble beginnings of a silicon wafer to the creation of a dense network of transistors and interconnects, the process is a masterpiece of engineering. It involves hundreds of meticulously orchestrated steps, executed with nanometer-level precision, all carried out in an environment so controlled that even a single speck of dust could spell disaster. Each phase, from photolithography to ion implantation, and from wafer testing to packaging, reflects the culmination of decades of scientific advancement, collaboration, and innovation.

Microchips are far more than mere components in our devices; they are the enablers of progress. These tiny marvels power the technologies that define modern life—smartphones, supercomputers, medical equipment, vehicles, and countless other innovations. Without microchips, the world as we know it would grind to a halt, bereft of the connectivity, efficiency, and computational power that drive our digital age. They are the unseen backbone of global industries, quietly transforming ideas into reality and enabling breakthroughs that shape the future.

Understanding how microchips are made is more than a technical exercise; it is an invitation to marvel at the ingenuity that powers our world. The intricate steps, the challenges of working at the nanoscale, and the collaboration of machines, materials, and minds—all of it inspires a deeper appreciation for the technology we often take for granted. Knowing the effort and expertise behind every chip fosters a sense of curiosity and respect for the unseen processes that fuel our devices.

This knowledge empowers us to view technology not as a black box of magic but as the product of human creativity and determination. It highlights the interconnection between science, industry, and innovation, reminding us that the tools we rely on daily are the result of countless hours of research, problem-solving, and meticulous craftsmanship. By exploring the world of microchip manufacturing, we gain a newfound respect for the extraordinary efforts that make the ordinary possible.

Microchips are more than just technological achievements; they are symbols of what humanity can accomplish when driven by curiosity, precision, and the desire to push boundaries. As we continue to advance, let this understanding inspire us to value the remarkable intersection of science and imagination that shapes our world, one nanometer at a time.